Phil H. LISTEMANN

Colour artwork: Claveworks Graphic

Layout & project design: Phil Listemann

Copyright © Philedition - Phil Listemann 2011
Revised - 2012

ISBN 978-2-9532544-7-1

All rights reserved. No parts of this publication may be reproduced, stored in a retrieval system or transmitted in any form or by any means, electronic, mechanical, photocopying, recording or otherwise, without permission in writing from the Authors.

Acknowledgements

C-J Ehrengardt, Lucien Morareau & ARDHAN (www.aeronavale.org),
Claude Requi (www.Frenchwings.net), Roger Wallsgrove (Text Consultant).

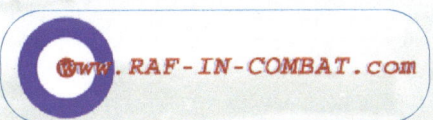

Edited and printed by Phil H. Listemann

philedition@wanadoo.fr

A SB2C-3 of VB-7 in January 1945. At that time, the Helldiver had already proved its efficiency, and was clearly a good combat aircraft. However, the concept of a pure dive-bomber was considered obsolete, explaining why the Helldiver was withdrawn from use within two years following VJ-Day. *(Author's collection)*

INTRODUCTION

The SB2C Helldiver was ordered on 15 May 1939. Actually it was the second Curtiss aircraft to have been christened like this and the biplane Curtiss SBC Helldiver was under production when its successor was ordered. The new aircraft was a low-wing monoplane with the same general layout as the Brewster SB2A Buccaneer, with which it was in competition. It was a two-seat scout-bomber powered by the big Wright R-2600 Double Cyclone engine, and had an internal bomb-bay in the fuselage. Comparing to the SBC, it was a big step forward.

The prototype XSB2C-l, with a 1,700 hp R-2600-8, made its first flight on 18 December 1940, but was destroyed a few days later. Large-scale production had already been ordered on 29 November 1940, but a large number of modifications were specified for the production mode!. The size of the fin and rudder was enlarged, fuel capacity was increased and self-sealing added, and the fixed armament was doubled to four 0.50-in guns in the wings, compared with the prototype's two cowling guns. Curtiss established a new factory for SB2C production at Columbus, Ohio, and the first production model did not fly until June 1942. After the first 200 SB2C-1s, fixed armament was again changed, this time to two 20-mm cannons installed in the SB2C-1C version; in addition the Helldiver had two 0.30-in guns in the rear cockpit, and its internal bomb load could reach 1,000 lb.

Although deliveries began in December 1942 the SB2C only went into action in November 1943. Production of the SB2C-1 totalled 978 which was followed by the SB2C-3, which began to appear in 1944 and had the R-2600-20 engine with a four-blade propeller, soon followed by the SB2C-4 which had wing fittings for eight 5-in rockets or up to 1,000 lb of bombs. Production by Curtiss amounted to 1,112 SB2C-3s and 2,045 SB2C-4s. Finally came 970 SB2C-5s, deliveries starting in February 1945, a version which had increased fuel capacity but few only were able to reach operational units before the war's end. The SB2C was also built under licence by two Canadian manufacturers as SBF (Fairchild, 300 built) and SBW (Canadian Car and Foundry, 894). A land-based version under the designation A-25 Shrike was also built, but was eventually rejected by the USAAF.

By 1944 the Helldiver was intensively used in the Pacific, replacing the Douglas SBDs Dauntless in the dive bombing role even it never totally replaced it. The needs of the USN were so huge that it kept nearly all the production for its units releasing only 26 Canadian-built aircraft supplied to Britain under Lend-Lease arrangements.

After VJ-Day, late versions of the Helldiver remained in US Navy service several years after the end of World War II, and many others were supplied to foreign countries like Greece, Portugal, Italy and France.

HELLDIVERS FOR THE FRENCH

By the time the French began to take on charge the SB2C, they had been involved in a bloody colonial conflict for almost four years. At the end of WW2, the French came back to Indochina which had been under Japanese domination during four long years. The political situation was however far from simple as the Japanese had granted independence to the natives of the region, natives who were also armed by the Americans to fight against the Japanese. Hence the return of the French was far from easy and talks started between the Nationalists and Communists on one side and the French on the other side to find an agreement. This came to an end in December 1946 when open conflict arose between the nationalist and communist forces and the French.

The French began the war with few and obsolete military weapons, mainly inherited from the USA with no support from the Americans who were against any kind of colonialism.

Things did not change until 1949 when China became a communist country. This was at the beginning of Cold war and China had become a major threat in the region to American interests, and anyone able to fight against the expansion of the Communism was welcomed. Thus in 1950, the French were not seen any more as a Colonial power only but also as part Free World country in the region fighting against Communism.

In 1949, the French Navy urgently needed new equipment for its aircraft-carriers and the ageing SBD Dauntless needed to be replaced. Naturally, the SB2C was selected because it was available in numbers from USN depots. Agreement rapidly reached with funds coming from the MDAP (Military Defense Assistance Pact).

The Curtiss Helldivers were delivered in several batches, the first of 56 aircraft being released to equip two combat units with aircraft held in reserve, but all were delivered in 1949-1950. Initial training took place at the USN base in Norfolk, where the first pilots and mechanics arrived in March 1950. These batches were followed by another 44 aircraft in 1952 as replacements and finally 10 more in 1955 to be used as components for the existing fleet. These were not included in the inventory although it is believed that at least two were put back to flying conditions. In all, the French Navy received 110 SB2C-5 Helldivers and they were used for a period of almost 10 years.

Curtiss SB2C known to have been used by French Navy

Bu.No.	USN	Stricken	French Navy	Bu.No.	USN	Stricken	French Navy
83196	30.03.45	28.02.49	11.02.52	89142	11.07.45	30.06.49	25.07.50
83228	07.04.45	28.02.49	19.05.50	89143	09.07.45	28.02.49	25.07.50
83239	06.04.45	28.02.49	19.05.50	89147	10.07.45	30.06.49	19.05.50
83247	10.04.45	31.05.49	28.04.52	89158	12.07.45	28.02.49	25.07.50
83259	12.04.45	28.02.49	19.05.50	89171	16.07.45	31.05.49	11.02.52
83269	13.04.45	28.02.49	17.04.50	89181	17.07.45	28.02.49	22.04.50
83293	19.04.45	28.02.49	17.04.50	89185	18.07.45	28.02.49	n/k
83312	21.04.45	28.02.49	17.04.50	89197	20.07.45	28.02.49	17.04.50
83326	24.04.45	28.02.49	17.04.50	89202	19.07.45	28.02.49	25.07.50
83332	26.04.45	28.02.49	17.04.50	89215	21.07.45	28.02.49	22.04.50
83333	25.04.45	28.02.49	17.04.50	89229	25.07.45	31.05.49	22.04.50
83335	25.04.45	31.05.49	17.04.50	89233	27.07.45	28.02.49	25.07.50
83341	26.04.45	28.02.49	17.04.50	89239	25.07.45	28.02.49	25.07.50
83358	01.05.45	28.02.49	25.07.50	89240	27.07.45	28.02.49	25.07.50
83368	03.05.45	31.03.49	11.02.52	89242	26.07.45	28.02.49	n/k
83395	05.05.45	28.02.49	27.04.50	89243	27.07.45	28.02.49	19.05.50
83396	05.05.45	30.06.49	19.10.50	89255	28.07.45	28.02.49	25.07.50
83403	12.05.45	28.02.49	18.05.50	89261	01.08.45	28.02.49	25.07.50
83412	08.05.45	28.02.49	18.05.50	89264	30.07.45	28.02.49	25.07.50
83444	15.05.45	28.02.49	22.04.50	89266	01.08.45	30.06.49	19.05.50
83447	14.05.45	31.05.49	28.04.52	89278	02.08.45	31.03.49	n/k
83450	14.05.45	28.02.49	n/k	89305	11.08.45	28.02.49	11.02.52
83472	17.05.45	28.02.49	25.07.50	89312	13.08.45	31.05.49	28.04.52
83482	19.05.45	30.06.49	n/k	89315	11.08.45	28.02.49	19.05.50
83504	23.05.45	28.02.49	22.04.50	89331	13.08.45	28.02.49	11.02.52
83544	29.05.45	28.02.49	25.07.50	89334	13.08.45	31.03.49	11.02.52
83545	01.06.45	28.02.49	28.04.52	89336	29.08.45	28.02.49	19.05.50
83558	02.06.45	28.02.49	n/k	89347	27.08.45	30.06.45	n/k
83566	02.06.45	28.02.49	25.07.50	89357	14.08.45	28.02.49	28.04.52
83580	07.06.45	31.05.49	28.04.52	89367	07.08.45	28.02.49	11.02.52
83581	06.06.45	28.02.49	25.04.52	89371	14.09.45	28.02.49	n/k
83599	11.06.45	28.02.49	n/k	89374	10.09.45	28.02.49	11.02.52
83611	08.06.45	28.02.49	27.04.50	89394	26.09.45	28.02.49	28.04.52
83616	12.06.45	28.02.49	19.05.50	89395	25.09.45	28.02.49	28.04.52
83626	13.06.45	31.05.49	28.04.52	89397	27.09.45	28.02.49	n/k
83633	16.06.45	28.02.49	11.02.52	89399	27.09.45	28.02.49	11.02.52
83668	21.06.45	30.06.49	28.04.52	89406	28.09.45	30.06.49	11.02.52
83687	23.06.45	28.02.49	28.04.52	89407	28.09.45	30.06.49	n/k
83689	25.06.45	31.05.49	28.04.52	89411	04.10.45	31.03.49	12.02.52
83693	25.06.45	30.06.49	19.05.50	89412	04.10.45	28.02.49	28.04.52
83730	03.07.45	30.09.49	19.05.50	89414	04.10.45	31.03.49	11.02.52
83731	02.07.45	28.02.49	n/k	89417	04.10.45	28.02.49	28.04.52
83732	28.06.45	30.09.49	n/k	89418	08.10.45	31.03.49	11.02.52
83736	28.06.45	28.02.49	n/k	89433	12.10.45	28.02.49	n/k
83737	05.07.45	28.02.49	19.05.50	89435	11.10.45	28.02.49	11.02.52
83745	03.07.45	30.06.49	n/k	89440	11.10.45	28.02.49	11.02.52
83746	05.07.45	30.06.49	25.07.50	89444	16.10.45	28.02.49	11.02.52
83751	06.07.45	31.05.49	11.02.52	89446	16.10.45	28.02.49	11.02.52
89121	07.07.45	31.05.49	28.04.52	89449	17.10.45	28.02.49	28.04.52
89123	07.07.45	28.02.49	n/k	89452	18.10.45	28.02.49	n/k
89135	07.07.45	31.05.49	28.04.52				

Helldivers of 3.F on the deck of the *Arromanches* during the battle of Dien Bien Phu in May 1954. The colonial conflict of Indochina was the last war in which the Helldiver participated.
(Meuinet via ARDHAN)

TECHNICAL DATA
SB2C-5

Manufacturer and production:
970 by Curtiss-Wright Corporation (Columbus, OH).

Type:
Carrier-based scout-bomber.

Accomodation:
Pilot, Observer-gunner.

Powerplant:
One Wright R-2600-20 fourteen-cylinder radial air-cooled
(2 rows) rated 1,900 hp.

Fuel & Oil
Fuel (US Gal):
Main tanks: 320 [1 456 l]
Auxiliary tanks: 304 [528 l]
Bomb bay tank: 130 [592 l]

Oil (US Gal):
Standard: 37.0 [140 l]

Dimensions:
Span: 49 ft 8.6-in [15,15 m]
Length: 36 ft 8-in [11,17 m]
Height: 13 ft 1.5-in [4,01 m]
Wing area: 422.0 Sq ft [39,19 m²]

Weights:
Empty: 10,580 lb [4 799 kg]
Gross: 15,918 lb [7 220 kg]
(Scout with one bomb-bay tank and one external tank)

Performance:
Max speed:
260 mph at 16,100 ft
[419 km/h à 4 900 m]

Cruising speed: 148 mph [238 km/h]

Service ceiling: 26,400 ft [8 050 m]

Normal range: 1,805 miles at 150 mph [2 905 km at 242 km/h]

Armament:
2 x 20mm cannon in the wings with 200 rpg

2 x 0.30-in [7.62mm] in rear cockpit with 1,000 rpg

provision for:
2,000 lb [908 kg] of bombs in the bomb bay and external

3.F-9 (Bu.No.83616) flying low preparing for deck landing on the *Arromanches* in 1951 during its first tour in Indochina. Contrary to the next colonial conflict in Algeria, the aircraft carrier played a vital role in the conduct of the war in the region, as did the American carriers a couple of years later.
(Choupin via ARDHAN)

THE UNITS

Flotille 3.F
code: 3.F
May 1950 - December 1954

The French Navy used the Helldiver in three first line units (*Flotille*). 3.F was one of the first two with 4.F anf 3.F became the unit which used the Helldiver in action the most. It had previously flown the SBD Dauntless with which it had participated in the first stages of the war in Indochina before being disbanded in 1948. 3.F was reformed on 1st May 1950 with SB2C-5s and *Lieutenant de Vaisseau* Bernard Waquet was selected to become its first CO. Training began nine days later and at this time the French Navy passed from Royal Navy procedures to USN procedures. In July 1951 3.F was selected to fly over the *Champs-Elysées* and it was actually the first time the Helldiver was officially shown to the French people. The same month, the *Flotille* received orders to prepare to go overseas for another tour in Indochina from the *Arromanches* and training was focused in the next few weeks on deck landing practice. On 28 August 1951, the *Arromanches* sailed with 12 SB2C-5s of 3.F and 18 F6F-5 Hellcats of 1.F, but unfortunately the number of aircraft parked on the deck prevented any more training which would have been useful for the crews of 3.F during the trip. The *Arromanches* with its Air Group arrived off Cap Saint-Jacques (later Vung Tau) on 24 September 1951 and some aircraft were disembarked at Tourane (later Da Nang) and Tan Son Nhut, 3.F keeping six Helldivers to conduct operations from the aircraft-carrier. Even before being engaged in any action, one Helldiver was lost by accident on 5 October (3.F-6/Bu.No.83482) fortunately without any serious injuries for the crew. The following day, the first missions were carried out against marshalling yards used by the Viêt-minh in central Anam, and between 14 and 21 October, the Air Group was acting in areas in Tonkin which were not under control of the French troops. It was during one such sortie on 17 October that the French suffered the first killed in action when 3.F-3 (Bu.No.83341) was shot down by A-A while attacking That Ke bridge. The two crewmen, *Lieutenant de Vaisseau* Gautriaud and *Second Maitre* Jean Jacq were killed in the crash. Although more powerful and more accurate than the Dauntless, it was often not enough to discourage the Viet-Minh to undertake repairs to restore many facilities in a very short time, obliging the French to return to previous targets more heavily defended than ever, a point the Americans would also learn a couple of years later...

Weather prevented any major operations until 14th November when the Helldivers were again called to provide air cover to the French troops engaged in Tonkin, for a period of a few days, around a week each time with a couple of days rest between. The *Arromanches* remained off the Tonkin coast until 9 January and the Helldivers were used as far as the weather permitted. Before the end of the month, the *Arromanches* was sent to Singapore for maintenance and during that time the crews continued their training, sometimes alongside Commonwealth units based in the area.

On 23 February 1952, the *Arromanches* returned to Cap Saint Jacques with a new CO for 3.F, *Lieutenant de Vaisseau* Lionel Marmier. Meanwhile the Helldivers based at Tan Son Nhut had been operated against the Viet-Minh and five aircraft were briefly engaged (Operation *Tourbillon*) in the south of the country alongside 16 Hellcats, where the hitting power of the Helldiver was duly appreciated. The *Arromanches* was sent again to the north coast off Tonkin and arrived on 6 March. The Helldivers were sent into action for the next two weeks. The weather was rather bad and made very difficult any mission and it was during the return journey from an operational sortie, that new 3.F-3 (Bu.No.89185) crashed whilst landing on the *Arromanches*, but the crew escaped without injuries. In March and April 1952, the Helldivers were involved in

Operation *Catapulte* against the roads heading to Laos usually used by the Viêt-Minh, performing 145 sorties in 14 days which include 4 days of bad weather. This air activity was not without accident when on 14 April a F6F Hellcat of 1.F (1.F-7) missed its landing on the deck of the *Arromanches* and crashed into the aircraft parked at the end of the deck, destroying six aircraft including one Helldiver (3.F-1/Bu.No.83269) and killing three sailors. During that time, the aircraft based at Tourane were also heavily engaged in action (Operation *Mimosa*) during the last week of March around Hue with subsequent results.

Air activity decreased between May and September because of the monsoon season and the heavy rains which increased the level of the rivers restraining consequently troop movements on both sides. Consequently, the *Arromanches* and its air group had no more reasons to stay in the area and was recalled to France, sailing on 18 May. It arrived on 13 June 1952 at Toulon while 3.F was disembarked at Hyères, its regular land base. During its tour, 3.F had performed over 400 sorties in 163 missions, dropped 530,000 pounds of bombs, fired 250 5" rockets and 85,000 rounds of ammunition, illustrating perfectly the intensity of the struggle in Indochina.

BACK IN INDOCHINA

While the *Arromanches* was sent back to Indochina with a new group carrier in October 1952, 3.F continued its training in France, from land bases or from the recently commissioned aircraft-carrier *La Fayette*. In summer 1953, 3.F was selected for a third tour in Indochina and on 7 September 16 Helldivers embarked on the *Arromanches* to the Far East, sailing with the Hellcats of Flotille 11.F. The Air Group arrived at Cat Bi on 29 September and the tactical group was disembarked at Tan Son Nhut to give a chance for the crews to carry on their training.

However the military situation soon obliged the Helldivers to be put into action in support of ground troops and other tasks, which included reconnaissance. On the 26 October, a new CO took over the *Flotille*, Lieutenant de Vaisseau Jean Andrieux. The Flotille was working on the basis of three weeks of operations, one week of rest, maintenance and supplies, and during autumn 1953, it was called to provide air support for Operations *Pélican* and *Mouette* over the Mekong Delta. Between 6 and 14 November, 3.F was active over the north (Tonkin), and on the 15th over the centre (Hué) near Dong Hoi - Operation *Réveil*. The following week, six SB2Cs were detached near Hanoi to provide air cover for Operation *Castor* which had the aim of occupying the Dien Bien Phu area by a mixed force of French and Vietnamese paratroopers. From that day, 3.F was regularly called to provide direct support to the Dien Bien Phu garrison, in striking the area as the Viêt-minh troops were beginning to converge to that place and many missions of interdiction were carried out especially against Road 41 in trying to prevent the Viet-Minh from reinforcing its troops around the strong point, but the Viêt-minh succeeded to close in and the garrison of Dien Bien Phu now became besieged. Operations continued the following weeks and increased week after week without losses in combat. However, intensive flak around the garrison increased steadily in February with the arrival of a fully-equipped Red Chinese AA regiment with 37mm cannons and plenty of other weapons like heavy machine-guns (12.7mm). Indeed with the termination of the Korean War, Communist China was able to send some gunners to help the Viêt-minh cause around Dien Bien Phu. The only loss 3.F sustained until mid-March was one Helldiver wrecked during an aircraft-carrier landing during a communication flight on the 4 March 1954 (3.F-15/Bu.No.83447), fortunately without injuries to the pilot.

Bu.No.89411/3.F.10 about to make its deck landing on the *Bois Belleau* in 1954. Note the the number '10' painted on the top of the fin, an unusual practice for the 3.F. *(Meulnet via ARDHAN)*

Helldivers of 3.F parked at Bach Mai (south of Hanoi) in 1954 at the early stage of the battle of Dien Bien Phu about to be re-armed. Helldiver 3.F-1 (probably Bu.No.89312) can be seen in the forefront. The Helldiver was intensively used over the area in 1954, but the struggle was actually lost from the beginning due to bad choices and underestimating the Viet-Minh's abilities in performing miracles! *(Joubert via ARDHAN)*

DIEN BIEN PHU

A couple of days later, during the night of the 13 and 14 March 1954, the Viêt-minh launched its great offensive against the strongpoint of Dien Bien Phu. The French garrison was rapidly put under pressure and air strikes were called up to try to release this pressure. The Helldivers were then detailed every day over the area, and priority were given to AA and artillery positions as far as they could be located, as they were a threat to any transport aircraft which wanted to land at the airstrip. On the 13th and 14th, one Helldiver was hit by AA fire but in both cases the aircraft was able to return to base (Bach Mai) and both were quickly repaired. The following day the first French strong out-post 'Gabrielle' felt to the enemy after a devastating bombardment and a massive assault by ground troops. The Helldivers tried to help the defences as far as they could but low clouds prevented any efficient attack and the impact on the enemy was insignificant. Indeed, what occurred on 15th was representative of what happened the following days; as far as the situation allowed, each aircraft was able to operate twice a day over their target, but the weather, especially a low cloud ceiling, obliged the French to cancel many sorties over the area. In face of such danger and to avoid unnecessary losses, 3.F decided not to embark the air gunner, leaving the pilot alone to complete the mission. It was a logical decision as during such missions the air gunner was rather useless. The Chinese A-A-A soon proved its efficiency when on the last day of March 1954, 3.F lost its CO, *Lieutenant de Vaisseau* Andieux, over Dien Bien Phu. The mission had started early in the the day, when four sections took off to provide air support to the French garrison but upon arriving over the target, clouds prevented any attack. They eventually found a hole in the layer of clouds but they were obliged to fly low and soon became within A.A.A range before reaching their target. The leader of the formation in 3.F-4 (Bu.No.89367) was hit and was set on fire, diving into the ground, crashing close to the strong point of 'Béatrice'. *Lieutenant de Vaisseau* Andrieux was temporary replaced by the *Lieutenant de Vaisseau* Hugues de Lestapis, the deputy commander.

The Flotille paid another toll to the Viet-Minh/Chinese A.A.A. nine days later when *Enseigne de Vaisseau* Jean-Marie Laugier was hit and killed over Dien Bien Phu (3.F-11/Bu.No.89334). After having dropped his bombs, the Helldiver was hit and Laugier was able to evacuate his aircraft, but too low to allow his chute to open. On 26 April, the *Flotille* was placed under

Lieutenant de Vaisseau Andrieux in his cockpit before being launched from the *Arromanches* off Indochina in 1954. He was killed a couple of days later over Dien Bien Phu.
(Andrieux family via ARDHAN)

the command of *Lieutenant de Vaisseau* Alain Fatou just before the unit was sent for a short rest on 3 May in board the *Bois Belleau* (ex-*USS Belleau Wood*), after almost eight weeks of intensive combat. It was replaced by the Corsair AU-1s of 11.F. Anyway the end was rapidly approaching for the French-Vietnamese troops at Dien Bien Phu, strongholds falling to the enemy one by one, the entire place falling eventually into Viet-Minh hands four days later. Since its arrival in the region, 3.F had achieved over 1,200 sorties, mostly in support of Dien Bien Phu. Air activity continued in May against the enemy ground troops which were now moving south. The unit was sent for rest in June only. It was also the time the unit was suffering serviceability problems, after weeks of intensive use, many aircraft needed maintenance and spares not always available.

END ON AN ERA

The fall of Dien Bien Phu boosted the Viet-Minh morale and with the arrival of more modern equipment, the Viet-Minh had become more dangerous than ever. In the meantime, the peace talks which had begun before the battle of Dien Bien Phu were accelerated and each one was trying to gain military advantages to be stronger around the peace talks table. Hence 3.F was sent again on operations in July, this time from the *Bois Belleau* but with less efficiency as the new crews which had replaced the first tour-expired ones were lacking training, preventing some of them from carrying out most of the important sorties. Finally, a cease-fire agreement was agreed and signed on 20 July, which was progressively put into force between 27 July (North), 1 August (Centre) and South (11 August). For the rest of Indochina the weapons finally ceased fire on on 6 August in Laos and the following day in Cambodia. For the carrier Air Group, all operations had stopped on 31 July. During this later stage, 3.F was still kept on alert and ready to carry out any war mission if needed, but this time was also used to complete the training of the newcomers even if it was done at low level. 3.F was finally disembarked and based at Tourane between 13 August and 29 September, as the *Bois Belleau* had been tasked to carry refugees from North to South and from South to North during those dates. However the presence of 3.F was soon deemed unecessary and all aircraft and personnel were repatriated to France on the transport ship *Dixmude* on 9 October, arriving at Toulon on 5 November. But with the war in Indochina over, France had to re-organise its military forces and, despite its impressive record, the French Navy decided to disband the unit on 31 December 1954.

Flotille 4.F
code: 4.F
May 1950 - April 1951

Flotille 4.F had been associated with dive-bombers for a long-time when it was selected to be equipped with SB2C Helldivers. It had previously used for many years the SBD Dauntless after the war until November 1949 when the unit was deactivated. In spring 1950 at the same time that *Flotille* 3.F was taking on charge its own Helldivers, six SB2Cs began to arrive at 4.F (Bu.Nos 83504, 83736, 89197, 89229, 89242 and 89407), soon followed by two others. Training was undertaken at once but under USN methods instead of the FAA methods used by the French Navy until that date. In July, all crews had become operational on the Helldiver. Despite this, the Helldiver remained only a short time with 4.F as the unit was selected to convert onto the TBM-3W Avenger recently bought from the USA, and the crews gave up their Helldivers in April 1951 after about 2,000 flying hours on the type, without recording any major accident. 4.F never had the opportunity to operate the Helldiver on operations.

Though 4.F was one of the first two units to convert onto the Helldiver, the *Flotille* switched to the Grumman TBM one year later without having used its Helldivers in operations. (*Nifenecker via ARDHAN*)

As the aircraft-carrier *Arromanches* was sent back to France for an overhaul, the 9.F and the 12.F (Hellcats) were based at Cat Bi in February 1953. The Helldivers of the 9.F are seen here on detachment at Nha Trang. (*Hevio via ARDHAN*)

Flotille 9.F
code: 9.F
June 1951 - June 1953

Flotille 9.F was the third and last unit to operate the SB2C. This unit, based at Karouba in Tunisia, was rather particular as it was previously equipped with Do24 flying boats when it began the conversion onto the Helldiver. Because of this past, conversion took more time compared to 3.F and 4.F. Crews were sent to France to receive training on the Helldiver and by June 1951, 9.F with 12 trained crews and eight Helldivers rejoined its base in Tunisia. The unit was soon reinforced in July with four more aircraft, with nine operational, the remaining three being held in reserve. Training continued the following months which sadly saw the loss of 9.F-3 (Bu.No.83412) on the 11 December and its pilot, *Enseigne de Vaisseau* Guy de Petyst Morcourt. 9.F embarked for the first time in April 1952 on board *La Fayette* and in August, 9.F sailed for Indochina on board *Arromanches*. After a stop-over at Djibouti and Sembawang (Singapore) the aircraft carrier arrived off Indochina on 28 September. The *Arromanches* sailed again a few days later, having left six Helldivers and four Hellcats at Tourane (Tan Son Nut) as reserve aircraft, and operations began on 8 October under the command of *Lieutenant de Vaisseau* J.C. Hervio, who had been appointed commanding officer the previous day. The first mission was against roads and bridges in the Than Hoa area and Vinh Hot. It wasn't long before 9.F lost its first Helldiver. On 15 October, Helldiver 9F-12 (Bu.No.89433) was destroyed just after being launched from the *Arromanches*, fortunately without serious injuries to the crew, captained by *Lieutenant de Vaisseau* Fatou.

Four days later, on 19 December 1952, 9.F recorded its first operational loss when 9.F-15 (Bu.No.89452) was lost without trace over the Laotian jungle in the Sam Neua region, the two crewmen, *Enseigne de Vaisseau* J. Paunet and *Second Maître* A. Lotodé being posted missing. Helldiver 9.F-15 had been sent for a reconnaissance sortie from Cat Bi airstrip and it was later discovered that they had hit a hill near Phou Nouei Cha for an unknown reason. In the beginning of 1953, the *Arromanches* left the area and sailed for Hong Kong, where she stayed between the 7th and the 13th of the month. On the 16th, the aircraft carrier was back on the Along Bay waters and operations were resumed the following days, sometimes from shore bases, like Nha Trang. The *Arromanches* was occasional-

9F-10 (89158) ready to be launched from the *La Fayette* in May 1952 for a dawn sortie off the coast of Indochina. (*Bourragué via ARDHAN*)

ly called to operate to the south and as the aircraft carrier was due to travel back to France for major overhaul, 9.F was disembarked and permanently based at Cat Bi from 17 February until the arrival of the *La Fayette* in the first days of April. Sorties were carried on from that land base, as far as the weather permitted air activity. After a short refresher training, air operations were resumed again from *La Fayette* on the 16 April, and the tour eventually ended at the end of May and 9.F returned to France on board *La Fayette*. During its tour, 9.F had flown 824 sorties and had dropped 1,442 tons of bombs and fired over 100,000 rounds of ammunition.

Arriving on 10 June at Toulon, the *Flotille* was disembarked and all its personnel sent on well-deserved leave. On their return from leave, the Helldivers had actually left and the unit was preparing to be converted onto the TBM Avenger, leaving 3.F alone to operate the Helldiver for the next few years.

Second Line Units

The Curtiss SB2C was of course used by various second line units during its career with the French Navy. The first of these was *Escadrille* 54.S which took charge of its five first Helldivers in May 1950. Its role was to train crews on the type for the operational units. The Helldivers were fully equipped during the first few months, but from November 1953 onwards, a part of their equipment was deleted, like the cannons, radar and tailhook, being totally unnecessary for the task. This 'lightweight' version flew with 54.S until March 1955, when the unit

The 10.S was at first in charge to try the Helldiver as ASM aircraft, but that proved not satisfactory. Later many other equipment was tried over 9 years period. This aircraft was wearing the unit insignia on the fin.
(Author's collection)

relinquished its last Helldiver. As with many training units, 54.S recorded some accidents. The worst occurred on 9 March 1953 when, during a IFR training flight, an aircraft developed some technical problem, white smoke then black appearing, later followed by flames, the aircraft losing height at the same time. The plane crashed a few seconds later killing two on board. *Escadrille* 10.S received its first Helldiver on charge as early as October 1950. This unit was a naval unit testing using various aircraft types. At that time, the French Navy had in mind to use the Helldiver in the ASM role, to save costs instead of purchasing a new type. However, this testing was not satisfactory,

Among the second line units, the 54.S based at Hyères near Toulon was probably the most important as its task was to train crews on the Helldivers. Here two Helldivers led by 54S.64 (Bu.No.83259) flying over the Mediterranean.
(Laurent Michel via ARDHAN)

Two SB2C-5s (Bu.No.83737 and 83444) of *Escadrille* 3.S flying over the French countryside. The 3.S was the Mediterranean area support flight based at Cuers near Toulon. (*Hesse via ARDHAN*)

and the idea was eventually rejected and TBM Avengers purchased instead. Later on, other Helldivers served with 10.S for other minor tests and the number decreased in the next few years and by 1958 only one remained on charge.

The Helldiver was also widely used by support units located at various French Navy areas, like 1.S (which became 2.S on 1 April 1955), 3.S in France and 4.S in Tunisia after 1955. All these units had to conduct various tasks, such as target-towing and training of various high ranking and reserve officers. Generally about six to seven Helldivers were used at the same time. Only few accidents were reported. On 23 January 1952, aircraft 3.S-8 (Bu.No.83558) was lost with its crew, *Enseigne de Vaisseau* Bernard Grisel and *Quartier Maître* Etienne Sliwinsk when, during an exercise with the Fleet, the Helldiver lost height and in a flat spin hit the sea. The crew could not be saved despite rapid searches carried out by the vessels around. Two years later, on 7 April 1954, 1.S-21 (Bu.No.89266) was obliged to make a force-landing into sea at Brest harbour, fortunately without injuries for the crew. However, even though the Helldiver was salvaged from the sea, it was declared beyond economical repair and struck off charge. As for 10.S, the Helldivers serving with the support units were progressively withdrawn and replaced by Grumman Avengers. By 1959, none was still flying with these units.

The SB2C served also in various naval station flights in France and North Africa as well aircraft carrier station flights, as for the *Bois Belleau* (coded BB-1 to BB-4) or *La Fayette* (coded LF-1 and LF-2) but in rather small numbers. Thus, a handful of Helldivers found their way to the Naval base of Karouba (Bizerte) in Tunisia but its size grew up so much that it was eventually renamed 4.S in 1955. The Helldiver disappeared from this unit when they were disbanded in 1956. At least one Helldiver was also used as personal mount of the Admiral commanding the Mediterranean area in 1952-1954.

The Helldiver served with the French during a period of 10 years or so. Its use was strongly connected with the war in Indochina and it did not participate in the next colonial war in Algeria, which began in 1954. Without this war in the Far East, the French may have selected others types for its aircraft-carriers, but the French had to go with what was available at low cost. With the war in this area over, the days were then counted for the Helldiver even if they found a useful way to serve in second lines units between 1955 and 1959. But this was possible because of the war in Algeria which became costly in many ways, and funds to replace and equip second lines units were more difficult to find out which delayed consequently the withdrawal of the Helldiver. But eventually the French did not regret this choice as the Helldiver did its job well in Indochina.

The end of the road for some Helldiver, which became instructional airframe at Rochefort. Here the number 5 (Bu.No.83745) which had been condemned in October 1952. (*C-J Ehrengardt*)

Aircraft-carrier *Bois Belleau* used 4 Helldivers coded BB-1 to BB-4 for about one year in its *Section de Servitude* (Station Flight) alongside two HUP-1s. Formed in December 1954, it was disbanded on 1 January 1956. (ARDHAN)

THE OPERATIONAL RECORD

Helldiver Bu.No.83580 sailing to Indochina in April 1954 on the *Bois Belleau*. This aircraft has no unit markings meaning that it was a replacement aircraft. Indeed, later on, it became 3.F-20. (*ARDHAN*)

AIR ACTIVITY OF *FLOTILLE* 3.F AND 9.F FROM AIRCRAFT CARRIER IN INDOCHINA

	Arromanches 1951-1952	Arromanches 1952-1953	La Fayette 1953	La Fayette 1953	Arromanches 08.10 to 28.11.53
Flotille	3.F	9.F	9.F	9.F & 12.F [1]	3.F
Operational hours	930	1362	257	774	978
Operational sorties	408	510	n/k	266	380
1,000-lb bombs	80	204	-	162	244
500-lb bombs	463	610	-	?	244
260 or 250-lb bombs	859	975	-	285	727
Clusters 6x20 or 3x23	30	178	-	157	45
Rockets 5"	250	344	-	249	168
Rockets 12"	-	-	-	?	-
20mm rounds	85,000	80,000	8,000	8,000	63,000
Napalm tanks (400 l)	8	-	-	131 (12.F)	-

[1] No separate figures are available. The 12.F was equiped with F6F Hellcat.

Aircraft Lost on Operations

Date	Unit	Crew	Bu.No.	Code	Fate
17.10.51	3.F	*Lieutenant de Vaisseau* Pierre Gautriaud	83341	3.F-3	†
		Second Maître Jean Jacq			†
08.03.52	3.F	*Enseigne de Vaisseau* Chatel	89185	3.F-3	-
19.12.52	9.F	*Enseigne de Vaisseau* Jacques Paunet	89452	9.F-15	†
		Maître André Lotodé			†
14.11.53	3.F	?	89687	3.F-11	-
04.03.54	3.F	*Lieutenant de Vaisseau* Duvillier	83447	3.F-15	-
31.03.54	3.F	*Lieutenant de Vaisseau* Jean Andrieux	89367	3.F-4	†
09.04.54	3.F	*Enseigne de Vaisseau* Jean-Marie Laugier	89334	3.F-11	†
20.07.54	3.F	*Maître* J.C. Mignot	89143	3.F-2	-
		Second Maître Claude Kolher			-

TOTAL: 8

Pierre Gautriaud. (*ARDHAN*)

Jean Jacq. (*ARDHAN*)

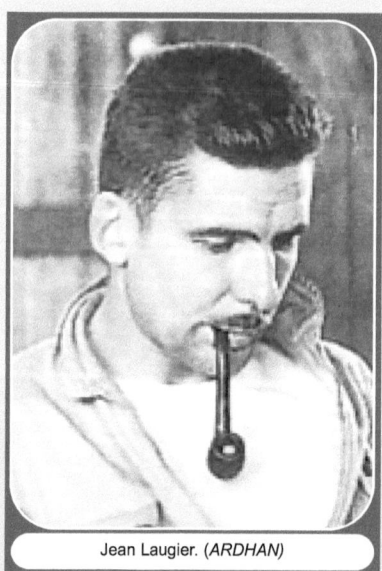

Jean Laugier. (*ARDHAN*)

Aircraft known to have been lost by Accident

Date	Unit	Crew	Bu.No.	Code	Fate
05.10.51	3.F	?	83482	3.F-6	-
		?			-
06.10.41	3.F	*Enseigne de Vaisseau* Choupin	83269	3.F-1	-
		?			-
11.12.51	9.F	*Enseigne de Vaisseau* Guy Petyst de Morcourt	83412	9.F-3	†
23.01.52	3.S	*Enseigne de Vaisseau* Bernard Grisel	83558	3.S-8	†
		Quartier Maître Etienne Slivinski			†
14.04.52	3.F	-	89123	3.F-1	-
26.04.52	54.S	?	89293	?	-
22.07.52	?	?	89278	?	-
19.08.52	9.F	?	89397	?	-
15.10.52	9.F	*Lieutenant de Vaisseau* Alain Fatou	89433	9.F-12	-
		?			-
11.02.53	3.F	?	83239	3.F-18	-
09.03.53	54.S	*Lieutenant de Vaisseau* Jean Milhé	83581	54.S-14	†
		Ingénieur Mécanicien Claude Dujardin			†
19.11.53	3.S	*Second Maître* Christian d'Estrées	83566	3.S-10	†
		Maître Roger Thomas			†
07.04.54	1.S	?	89266	1.S-21	-
23.04.54	3.F	?	83368	3.F-5	-
21.12.54	SEA[1]	?	89444	?	-
06.06.55	3.F	?	89395	?	-
27.10.55	3.S	?	83472	?	-
14.06.56	SEA	?	83751	?	-

[1]: SEA: *Section d'Atelier d'Aéronefs* (Aircraft Workshop Unit)

Total: 18

Guy Petyst de Morcourt. (*ARDHAN*)

Jean Milhé. (*ARDHAN*)

KNOWN ALLOCATIONS and CODES

Bu.No.

83196: **9.F-1** (1952-1953), **3.F-22** (1954)
83238: **9.F-5** (1951), **9.F-6** & **9.F-7** (1952-1953)
83239: **3.F-18** (1952)
83247: **3.F-7** (1953), **3.F-2** (1954), **3.S-6** (1957)
83259: **54.S-64** (1950 - 1951), **3.F-10** (1952)
83269: **3.F-14** (1951) then **3.F-1** (1951)
83293: **54.S-61** (1951)
83312: **3.F-2** (1951), *54.S*
83326: **3.F-7** (1950)
83332: **9.F-11** (1951)
83333: *54.S*
83335: **3.F-9** (1950)
83341: **3.F-3** (1951)
83358: **3.F-4** then **3.F-16** (1951), **3.F-4** (1952)
83368: *54.S* (1952), **3.F-5** (1954)
83395: **3.F-1** (1950), **3.F-5** (1952), **9.F-2** (1953)
83396: **3.F-8** (1950), **3.S-6** (1951)
83403: **3.F-3** (1951), **1.S-22** (1951-1953), **54.S-15** (1954)
83412: **4.F-3** (1950), **9.F-5** then **9.F-3** (1951)
83444: **3.F-4** (1950), **3.S-4** (1952 - 1953)
83447: **3.F-15** (1954)
83450: **3.F-10** (1951)
83472: *3.F*, **3.S-5** (1955)
83482: **3.F-13** (1951) then **3.F-6** (1951)
83504: *4.F* (1950), **3.F-17** (1951-1952)
83544: **3.F-5** (1951), **3.S-7** (1953)
83545: **3.F-18** (1953)
83558: **3.F-2** (1950), **3.S-8** (1952)
83566: **3.F-8** (1952), **3.S-10** (1953)
83580: **3.F-20** (1954)
83581: **3.F-7** (1952), **54.S-14** (1953)
83599: **9.F-12** (1951)
83611: **3.F-5** (1950), *54.S* (1952)
83616: **3.F-9** (1952)
83626: **3.F-6** (1953), **3.F-21** (1954)
83633: **3.F-5** (1953), *2.S* (1957)
83668: **3.F-9** (1954)
83687: **3.F-11** (1953)
83689: **3.F-7** (1953)
83693: **3.F-11** (1951), **3.F-12** (1952)
83730: **4.F-8** (1950), **9.F-8** (1951), **3.S-9** (1952), **3.S-4** (1953), **10.S-10** (1953), **10.S-31** (1955)
83731: **3.F-1** (1950)
83732: **9.F-7** (1951), **3.F-6** (1952)
83736: **4.F-2** (1950), **9.F-2** (1951), **3.F-1** (1953)
83737: **54.S-66** (1950 - 1951), **3.F-2** (1952)
83745: **3.F-6** (1950), **3.F-10** (1951)
83746: *3.F*
83751: **3.F-27** (1954), **3.S-6** (1955)
89121: **3.F-12** (1953)
89123: **3.F-1** (1952)
89135: **10.S-24** (1952), **10.S-6** (1953)
89142: **3.F-15** (1952), *2.S* (1957)
89143: **3.F-2** (1953)
89147: **3.F-17** (1952)
89158: **9.F-10** (1951-1953), *3.S* (1955)

89171: **54.S-17** (1953), **3.S-4** (1954)
89181: **3.F-3** (1950), **54.S-65** (1952)
89185: **3.F-3** (1952)
89197: *4.F* (1950), **9.F-6** (1951)
89202: **3.F-15** (1951), **3.F-11** (1952), **BZ.21** (1953), **4.S-21** (1955)
89215: *4.F* (1950), *54.S* (1951), *3.S* (1953)
89229: *4.F*, **1.S-21** (1954)
89233: *54.S*, **3.F-16** (1952), **3.S-8** (1957)
89239: **9.F-9** (1951), **3.S-6** (1955)
89240: **3.F-12** (1951 - 1952), *3.S* (1955)
89242: *4.F* (1950)
89243: **10.S-10** (1950?), **10.S-22** (1951-1953) then **10-S.7** (1953)
89255: **10.S-24** (1952) then **10.S-23** and **10.S-8**, *2.S* (1957)
89261: **3.F-4** (1951), **1.S-20** (1951-1954), *4.S* (1955)
89264: *4.F* (1950), **54.S-60** (1953)
89266: **3.F-12** (1950), **1.S-21** (1951-1953)
89278: **1.S-23** (1952)
89305: **9.F-13** (1952),
89312: *54.S*, **3.F-1** (1953)
89315: **9.F-4** (1951), *3.F* (1952), *4.S* (1955)
89331: **9.F-9** (1952), **3.F-6** (1953)
89334: **9.F-6** (1952), **3.F-11** (1953)
89336: **4.F-4** (1950), **9.F-1** (1951), **3.S-5** (1952)
89347: *Never issued to any unit.*
89357: **3.F-16** (1953 - 1954)
89371: *Never issued to any unit.*
89374: **9.F-8** (1952), **3.F-25** (1954)
89394: **9.F-14** (1952), **3.S-6** (1952), **3.F-24** (1954)
89395: **9.F-2** (1952)
89397: **9.F-7** (1952)
89399: **3.F-40** (1954)
89406: **9.F-11** (1952 - 1953), **3.F-28** (1954)
89407: **4.F-3** (1950)
89411: **3.F-10** (1954)
89412: **9.F-5** (1952 - 1953), **3.F-17** (1954)
89414: **3.S-8** (1952)
89417: **3.F-8** (1954)
89418: **54.S-9** (1952), **3.F-29** (1954)
89433: **9.F-12** (1952)
89435: **9.F-8** (1952), **1.S-20** (1953)
89440: **9.F-4** (1952 - 1953), **3.F-26** (1954)
89444: **9.F-3** (1952 - 1953), **3.S-4** (1953), **3.F-41** (1954)
89446: **3.F-14** (1954)
89449: **LF-2** (1953 - 1955)
89452: **9.F-15** (1952)

Above left, Bu.No.83196 9.F-1 seen at Sembawang (Singapore) on 29 September 1952 while en route to Indochina. This Helldiver was taken on charge by the French the previous February and was finally condemned in June 1958. (*ARDHAN*)

Above right, believed to be Bu.No.83247 coded 3.F-2 in Indochina in 1954. The last three digits '247' can be read behind the roundel. However this aircraft is reported to have been coded 3.F-7 while serving with 3.F in 1954. (*ARDHAN*)

Right: Shortly after being taken on charge by the French Navy, Bu.No.83293 was sent to 54.S at the Naval Air Base of Hyères to train crews on the type, where it is seen in 1951. It was damaged in a crash-landing after being short of fuel during a training flight on 26 April 1954. It was condemned four months later. (*ARDHAN*)

Below: Bu.No.83403 was among the batch of Helldivers used by 3.F in 1951 to work up on the type during the first half of 1951. It is seen here flying over the French coast off Hyères in June 1951 with the crew Duquesne/Guiraud on board. However this SB2C was not sent with the unit and was passed on to *Flotille* 1.S later that year, then 54.S (see next page). Its code 3.F-3 was taken over by Bu.No. 83341. (*ARDHAN*)

Left: Belly landing for Bu.No.83403 while serving with 54.S (5 May 1954). Its pilot, *Enseigne de Vaisseau* Joubert, escaped injury. The Helldiver was repaired and was condemned the following year on 19 November 1955. (*ARDHAN*)

Below: *Lieutenant de Vaisseau* Jean Andrieux, flying with Bu.No.83566/3.F-8 over the countryside of Indochina in March 1952 during the first tour of 3.F on Helldivers. Upon return from this tour, 83566 was passed on to *Flotille* 3.S and was lost during a training flight off Hyères on 19 November 1953. (*ARDHAN*)

Bottom - left: Before serving with 54.S in 1953, Bu.No. 83581 served briefly with *Flotille* 3.F in 1952. As with 83566 it was eventually lost in a flying accident in March 1953. (*ARDHAN*)

Bottom - right: Bu.No.83599 of 9.F was damaged in a deck-landing accident on the *La Fayette* on 9 May 1952. The Helldiver was repaired and ended its life as instructional airframe at Rochefort coded '1' in 1955. (*ARDHAN*)

Right: Right: Deck landing accident for 3.F-11 (Bu.No.83693) in 1951. The aircraft was repaired and survived until April 1955 when it was condemned. Note that in the early years of service, the French Helldivers wore the last three digits of the Bu.No behind the roundel. (*ARDHAN*)

Below: 3.F-5 (Bu.No.83633) leading a formation in Indochina in February 1954 during a routine flight. It was condemned in October 1957.
(*Jean Moulin via ARDHAN*)

Bottom: 9.F-2 (Bu.No.83736) taken during a training flight off Karouba (Tunisia) at the end of 1952. Note that the wing roundel has not the Navy anchor painted on, as well the absence of the unit insignia on the tail.
(*M. Laurent via ARDHAN*)

Top left: Top left: Flying formation for 9.F in 1951 off Karouba (Tunisia). Aircraft 9.F-2 is Bu.No.83736. (Bourragué via ARDHAN)

Top right: Bu.No.83737 coded 54.S-66 in 1951. Note the high sequence number regularly used by second line units. (Jacobi via ARDHAN).

Upper left: Nice shot showing Bu.No.83745 off the French coast in December 1950. The aircraft was later condemned to become instructional airframe No.5 at Rochefort in 1952. (Nifenecker via ARDHAN)

Above: Another training flight for 54.S-17 (Bu.No.89171) off Hyères on 18 December 1953. The Bu.No. is now painted in full just below the tailplane. (Muinet via ARDHAN)

Right: Bu.No.89158 served for two years with Flotille 9.F as 9.F-10, including in Indochina. It was later used by Flotille 3.S. (Author's collection)

Left: One of the Helldivers used by the Karouba (Tunisia) Station Flight in 1953. BZ.21 was actually Bu.No.89202. (*ARDHAN*)

Below: Bu.No.89243 was never issued to any operational unit, and probably served with 10.S only. It is known that it was used to test the Helldiver as an ASM aircraft. During its stay at 10.S, it wore at least three identifications, 10.S-7, 10.S-10 and 10.S-22. It was probably the last Helldiver in service when it was condemned in January 1959. (*ARDHAN*)

Left: Bu.No.89261/3.F-4 on finals at Hyères in mid-1951. It later served with Flotille 1.S between 1951 and 1954 before being condemned. (*Author's collection*)

Below: Bu.No.89264/54.S-60 taxiing in 1953. It was eventually condemned in 1955 and served on a dump to train Navy firemen. (*Claude Requi - Frenchwings.net*)

Left: Bu.No.89266/3.F-12 taxiing while with 3.F in 1951. Soon after it was passed on to *Flotille* 1.S and was lost in an accident on 7 April 1954 after engine failure in the circuit over Lann-Bihoué, making an emergency landing in Brest harbour. The aircraft was salvaged but not repaired.
(Author's collection)

Below: Bu.No.89315/9.F-4 seen off Karouba in 1951 showing both sides. No unit insignia can be seen on this aircraft. This Helldiver ended its life as instructional airframe No.3 at Rochefort in 1957.
(Bourragué via ARDHAN)

Bottom: Bu.No.89331/3.F-6 in May 1954 parked without ordnance at Bach Mai (Indochina). At that time the *Flotille* was located at four different places, the *Arromanches*, Bach Mai, Cat Bi and *Bois Belleau*.
(Fournier via ARDHAN)

Above: *Flotille* 4.F was the first to be equipped on Helldivers but flew them for only a short time between April 1950 and April 1951. Here Bu.No.89336 flying over the south east of France during a training flight. It was later used by 1.F and 3.S before being condemned in December 1954 to become an instructional airframe at Rochefort. (*ARDHAN*)

Left: Helldiver 3.F-6 seen in Indochina in 1953-1954. This number was allocated to Bu.No.89331 and was used during the second tour of 3.F in Indochina.
(*Author's collection*)

Below: Bu.No.89357/3.F-16 at Bach Mai in 1954 ready for another sortie with its full load of HVAR rockets installed on their racks. Note the new 3.F badge painted on the fin.
(*Fournier via ARDHAN*)

Above: *Lieutenant de Vaisseau* Jean Andrieux in 3.F-4 (Bu.No.89367) flying over Indochina in October 1953 during the beginning of the second tour of 3.F in the area. Andrieux was eventually shot down and killed whilst flying this aircraft on 31 March 1954 over Dien Bien Phu. Note that no full or partial Bu.No. is visible, a practice which seems to have been common for 3.F during the tour of 1953-1954. (*Andrieux via ARDHAN*)

Below left: During the tour of 9.F in Indochina in 1952, the number '11' was allocated to Bu.No.89406. This Helldiver completed another tour in Indochina with 3.F in 1954 as 3.F-28 and survived to become instructional airframe '6' at Rochefort in 1956. Note that 9.F had to paint the individual number on the fin.
(*Author's collection*)

Below right: Bu.No.89411/3.F-10 seen in Indochina in during the second tour of 3.F in Indochina, armed with two 1,000-lb bombs under the wings. This Helldiver returned to France at the end of the tour, but was condemned a few weeks later in February 1955. Note that the insignia painted on the fin is not the 3.F badge but more probably the badge of Karouba Naval Station. The mechanics didn't have time or the will to make the change! (*Author's collection*).

Above: After a first tour with 3.F as 3.F-8 in 1951-1952, Bu.No.89435 was issued to Flotille 1.S later on. It was one of the six Helldivers allocated to 1.S in 1954. It was finally withdrawn from use in December 1956. (*ARDHAN*)

Left: 9F.4 (Bu.No.89440) and 9.F-7 (Bu.No.83238) in flight over Indochina during the tour of 9.F in the area. Bu.No.89440 returned safely to France and completed another tour in South East Asia in 1954 with 3.F. However, if it survived for second time, it was condemned upon arrival back in France as being war-weary. Note the style of the individual number used by the unit. (*ARDHAN*)

Bottom: Another 9.F Helldiver on patrol around Nha Trang in 1952. 9.F-15 was Bu.No.89452 which was lost later during an armed recce over Laos on 19 December 1952, the crew being reported missing. (*ARDHAN*)

ROLL OF HONOUR

Name	Rank	Date	Bu.No.
ANDRIEUX, Jean Dominique	EV	31.03.54	89367
D'ESTRÉE, Christian Ferdinand Charles	SM2	19.11.53	83566
DUJARDIN, Claude René André	IM3	09.03.53	83581
GAUTRIAUD, Pierre Maurice Jean	LV	17.10.51	83341
GRISEL, Bernard André	EV1	23.01.52	83558
JACQ, Jean François Marie	SM1	17.10351	83341
LOTODÉ, André Fernand Henri	Mt	19.12.52	89452
MILHÉ, Jean Georges	LV	09.03.53	83581
PAUNET, Jacques Lucien	EV1	19.12.52	89452
PETYST de MORCOURT, Guy	EV1	11.12.51	83412
SLIVINSKI, Étienne	QM2	23.01.52	83558
THOMAS, Roger André Louis	Mt	19.11.53	83566

Total: 12

Helldiver BB.3 of *Bois Belleau* Station Flight about to be launched in July 1955. (*Michaulet via ARDHAN*)

Curtiss SB2C-5 Bu.No.83405, *Flotille* 3.F, Hyères (France), Summer 1951.
The note the 3.F insignia painted on the fin without its crest, and the style of last three digits of the Bu.No.
(see photo p.17)

Curtiss SB2C-5 Bu.No.83367, *Flotille* 3.F, *Lieutenant de Vaisseau* Jean Andrieux, Indochina, October 1953.
(see photo p.24)

Curtiss SB2C-5 Bu.No.83633, *Flotille* 3.F, Indochina, February 1954.
(see photo p.19)

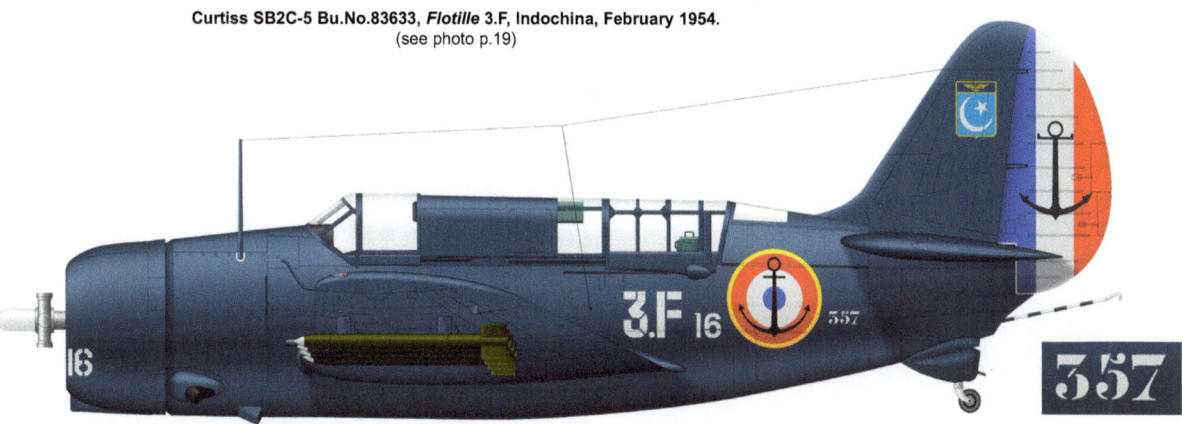

Curtiss SB2C-5 Bu.No.89357, *Flotille* 3.F, Bach Maï, Indochina, 1954.
(see photo p.23)

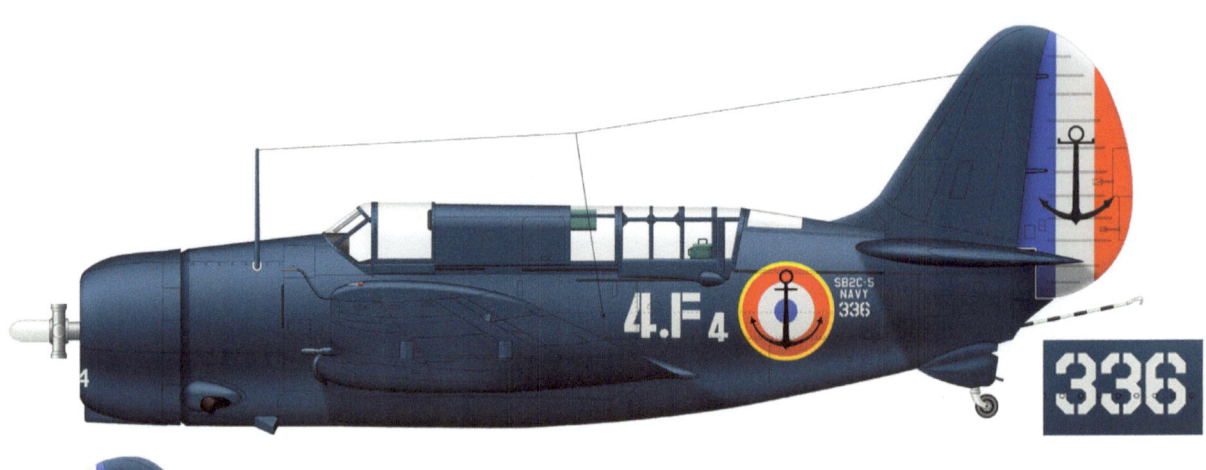

Curtiss SB2C-5 Bu.No.89336, *Flotille* 4.F, Hyères (France), 1950-1951.
(see photo p.8)

Curtiss SB2C-5 Bu.No.83736, *Flotille* 9.F, Karouba (Tunisia), 1952.
Note the small sized anchor painted on the rudder. (see photo p.19)

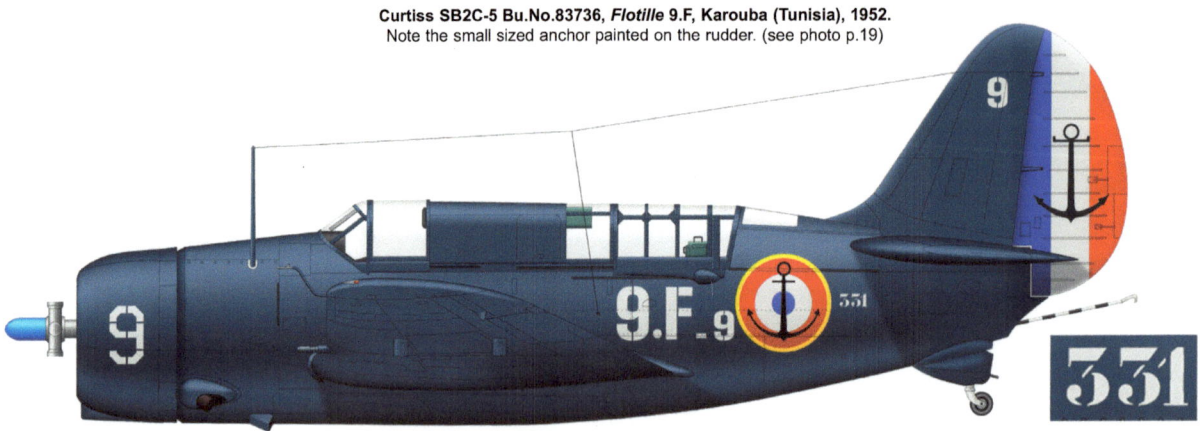

Curtiss SB2C-5 Bu.No.89331, *Flotille* 9.F, Indochina, 1952-1953.
The aircraft of the 9.F used to have their individual numbers painted on the fin and on cowling.

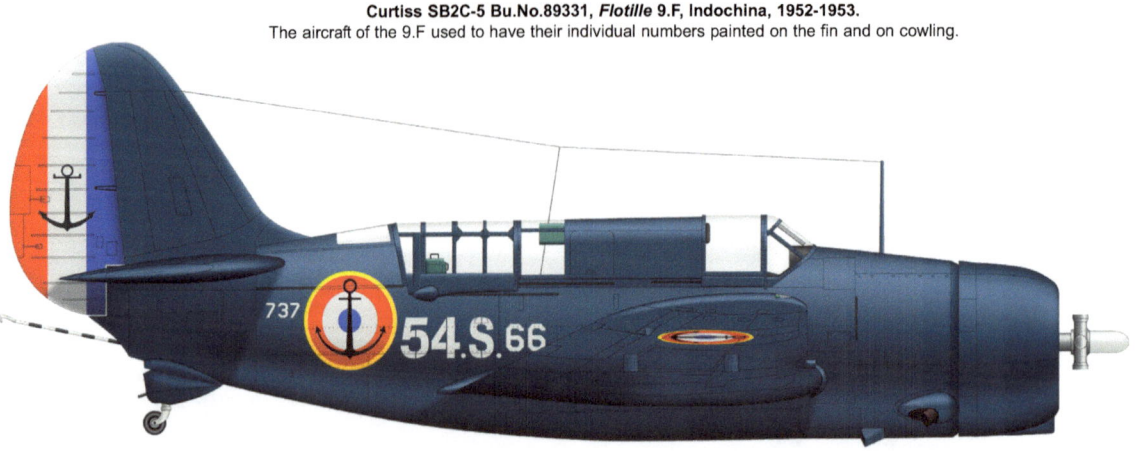

Curtiss SB2C-5 Bu.No.89171, *Escadrille* 54.S, Hyères (France), 1953.

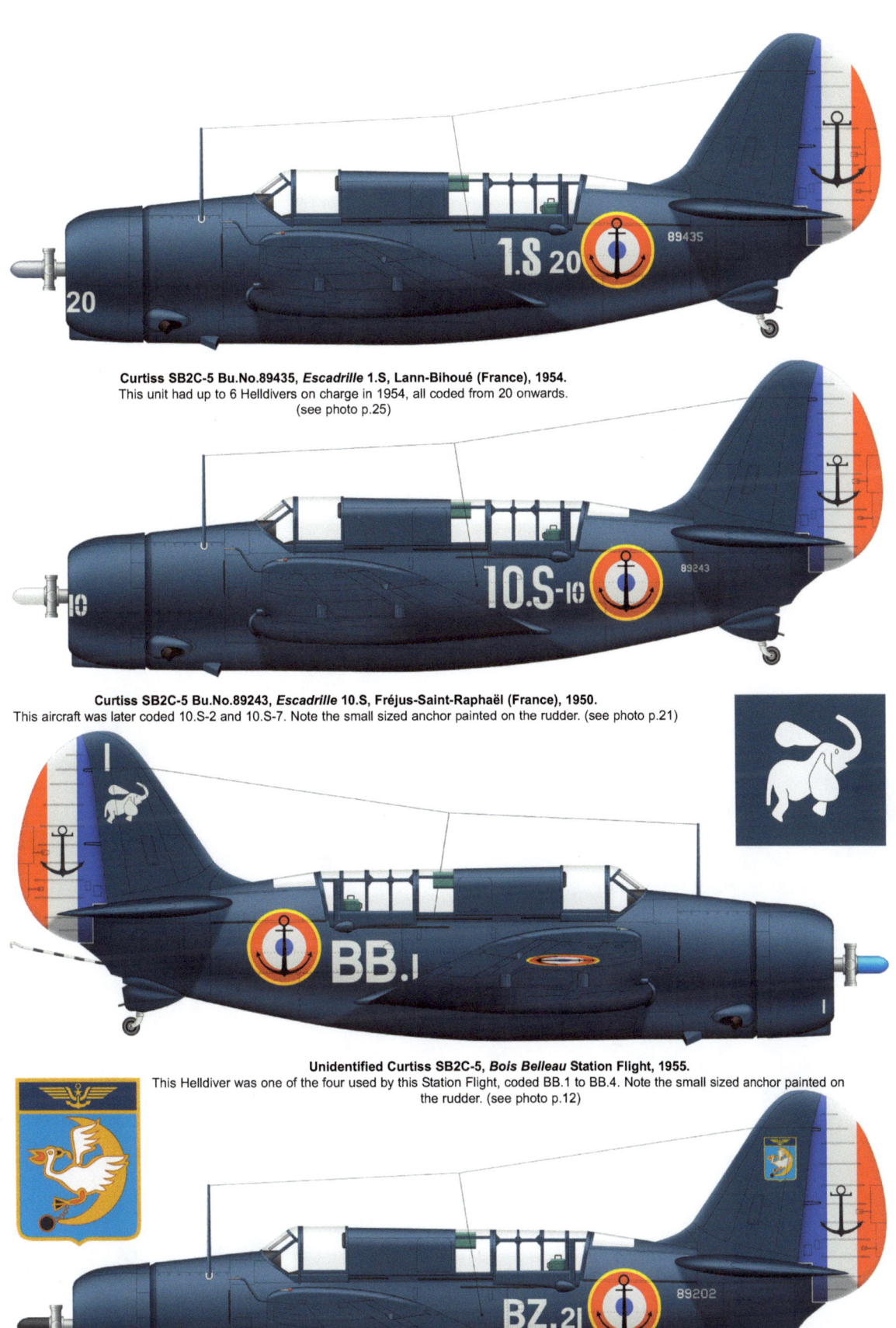

Curtiss SB2C-5 Bu.No.89435, *Escadrille* 1.S, Lann-Bihoué (France), 1954.
This unit had up to 6 Helldivers on charge in 1954, all coded from 20 onwards.
(see photo p.25)

Curtiss SB2C-5 Bu.No.89243, *Escadrille* 10.S, Fréjus-Saint-Raphaël (France), 1950.
This aircraft was later coded 10.S-2 and 10.S-7. Note the small sized anchor painted on the rudder. (see photo p.21)

Unidentified Curtiss SB2C-5, *Bois Belleau* Station Flight, 1955.
This Helldiver was one of the four used by this Station Flight, coded BB.1 to BB.4. Note the small sized anchor painted on the rudder. (see photo p.12)

Curtiss SB2C-5 Bu.No.89202, *S.E.S* Bizerte-Karouba (*Section d'entraînement et de Servitude of Karouba* - Station Flight*)*, Tunisia, 1953.
This aircraft was one of the two used by the Station Flight, the other being coded BZ.20. Note theon the fin, the Karouba base insignia.
Note the small sized anchor painted on the rudder. (see photo p.21)